CAPTAIN MACDONALD'S ARTILLERY DRESS ALBUM 1625-1897

A series of watercolour sketches illustrating the dress of the Regiment

THE DRUM MAJOR OF THE ROYAL REGIMENT OF ARTILLERY.
Circa 1840.

CAPTAIN MACDONALD'S ARTILLERY DRESS ALBUM 1625-1897

A series of watercolour sketches illustrating the dress of the Regiment

Compiled and Illustrated by

CAPTAIN R. J. MACDONALD, R.A.

The Naval & Military Press Ltd

Published by

The Naval & Military Press Ltd
Unit 10 Ridgewood Industrial Park,
Uckfield, East Sussex,
TN22 5QE England

Tel: +44 (0) 1825 749494
Fax: +44 (0) 1825 765701

www.naval-military-press.com
www.military-genealogy.com

In reprinting in facsimile from the original, any imperfections are inevitably reproduced and the quality may fall short of modern type and cartographic standards.

LIST OF COLOURED PLATES.

FRONTISPIECE.—Drum-Major of the Royal Regiment of Artillery ... ... circa 1840

PLATE No. 1. Train of Artillery 1660–1702
2. Train of Artillery 1702–1714
3. Royal Artillery 1743
4. Royal Artillery 1760
5. Royal Artillery 1764
6. Royal Artillery 1778
7. Royal Horse Artillery 1793
8. Royal Artillery 1794
9. Royal Artillery 1797
10. Royal Artillery 1799
11. Royal Horse Artillery 1815
12. Royal Horse Artillery (Rocket Troop) 1815
13. Royal Artillery 1815
14. Royal Artillery 1820
15. Royal Horse Artillery 1823
16. Royal Horse Artillery 1828
17. Royal Artillery 1828
18. Royal Artillery 1840
19. Royal Horse Artillery 1850
20. Royal Artillery 1854
21. Royal Horse Artillery 1855
22. Royal Artillery 1864
23. Royal Horse Artillery 1893
24. Royal Artillery 1897

Plate I.

AN OFFICER AND ARTILLERYMAN OR MATROSS, TRAIN OF ARTILLERY.

1660—1702.

Description of Plate.

The figure on the left depicts an Officer of the Train of Artillery during this period. He wears the large felt hat and feathers which succeeded the helmet of steel, but generally a small steel cap was sewn inside the hat for protection from sabre-cuts.

The hair was worn curled, falling on the shoulders, and generally ending in two love-locks; but during the reigns of James II. and his successors down to George II., perukes were worn, which were made of false hair to imitate long waving curls.

The steel cuirass was still worn, and was discontinued about the time George I. came to the throne. At this time it was the custom to wear it outside the coat.

The boots of the period were of that large heavy kind called "gambadoes," having very large tops to them, to prevent the leg being crushed in a charge.

On the right is shown an artilleryman or matross, carrying his linstock, with which to fire the gun.

He wears a broad belt or girdle round his waist of neat's leather, from which depends his brass-hilted hanger or cutlass, and across his shoulders is slung a powder-horn and a pouch or wallet.

Our soldiers, up to the time of Frederick the Great, always stood on parade, when at the position of attention, with their legs apart.

Authorities.—"History of the British Standing Army, A.D. 1660-1700." By Colonel Clifford Walton, C.B.
    Cleaveland's "Notes on the Early History of the Royal Artillery."
    Grose's "Military Antiquities."
    Meyrick's "Antient Armour."
    Luard's "History of the Dress of the British Soldier."
    Details, Colours.—Warrant 1689, signed by Schomberg for gunners, etc.
    Style of Dress, etc.—Van Wyck's "Boyne;" Mallet, "St. Remy," etc.
    Arms and Accoutrements.—In Brit. Mus. Add. MSS. 5795. In Harl. MSS. 7458-63, States of Ordnance Stores, 1687-91, appear, "powder-horns and linstocks for matrosses, and girdles of neat's leather with brass buckles for bombardiers."
Note.—The matrosses' and gunners' swords formed a portion of the clothing. Orders for dress as quoted in text.

TRAIN OF ARTILLERY
1660-1702.

PLATE II.

AN OFFICER, TRAIN OF ARTILLERY.

1702—1714.

Description of Plate.

This plate represents an Officer of high rank in the Train of Artillery during Marlborough's wars on the continent. He wears a cuirass under his long coat, encircled by a crimson sash; the large cavalry boots called gambadoes, with silver spurs.

A three-cornered laced cocked hat was worn; also a large peruke.

Authorities.—Grose's "Military Antiquities."
Luard's "History of the Dress of the British Soldier."
Portrait of General Borgard, R.A. Circa 1710.
Portrait of Colonel Jonas Watson, R.A. Circa 1710.
Portrait of Captain John Romer, Engineers. 1710.
Orders for dress as quoted in text previously.

TRAIN OF ARTILLERY.

1702-1714.

PLATE III.

AN OFFICER AND GUNNER, ROYAL ARTILLERY.

1743.

DESCRIPTION OF PLATE.

THIS represents a typically Georgian style of dress.

The figure on the left is an Officer, and on the right is a gunner, of the period.

The Officer carried as arms a fusee and gold-hilted sword. His crimson silk sash was very long and broad, having a hole at each end. A pole could be run through the two ends, and a hammock formed in which to carry the Officer off the field if wounded.

The description in detail of the dress of both Officer and gunner is given on pp. 22, 23.*

* See Order of Dress, Kane's List.

AUTHORITIES.—Two Water-colour Sketches in "The Cloathing of H.M. Forces." 1743. Orders for Dress as quoted in text.

ROYAL ARTILLERY.

1743.

Plate IV.

AN OFFICER OF THE ROYAL ARTILLERY.

1760.

Description of Plate.

This was the style of dress worn at Minden, and differed but slightly from the uniform of 1743.

Officers still carried fusees.

The gorget signified that the Officer was on duty, and was worn over the waistcoat.

Authorities.—Engraving, "Portrait of Captain Tiffin, R.A., at Minden."
Portrait of Colonel Griffiths Williams, R.A. Circa 1760.
Portrait of Thos. Hosmer, R.A. Circa 1760.
Orders for dress as quoted in text.

ROYAL ARTILLERY.

1760.

PLATE V.

AN OFFICER OF THE ROYAL ARTILLERY.

1764.

DESCRIPTION OF PLATE.

SINCE the date of the last plate, the colour of the waistcoat and breeches was changed from scarlet to buff; otherwise the style of the dress remained unaltered.

AUTHORITIES.—Portrait of Captain John Godwin, R.A. Circa 1764.
    Miniature of an Officer R.A. (no name or date). Circa 1764.
    Orders for dress as quoted in text.

ROYAL ARTILLERY.

1764.

PLATE VI.

AN OFFICER OF THE ROYAL ARTILLERY.

1778.

DESCRIPTION OF PLATE.

WHITE waistcoats and breeches were now worn; sashes, round the waist, instead of diagonally over the shoulder. The uniform was less cumbrous than heretofore.

AUTHORITIES.—Portrait of Captain Patterson, R.A. Circa 1778.
Portrait of Colonel Stehelin, R.A. Circa 1778.
Pencil sketch of an Officer R.A. 1778.
Miniature of an Officer R.A. (no name or date). Circa 1778.
Orders for dress as quoted in text.

ROYAL ARTILLERY.

1778.

PLATE VII.

AN OFFICER OF THE ROYAL HORSE ARTILLERY.

1793.

Description of Plate.

Horse Artillery was introduced into the British Army in 1793, the two first troops, A and B, being formed in that year.

The plate shows an Officer of the "Chestnut Troop," in the uniform worn at that date (*vide* Plate XXIII. for centenary).

The hair is worn in a small queue, tied with a few turns of ribbon, and ornamented with a large silk rosette. Both Officers and men used powder.

The head-dress worn was a helmet, similar to the old English Light Dragoon helmet. The turban or fillet surrounding the lower part was of crimson silk; white plumes were worn on the left side of it.

The first Horse Artillery jacket was after the style of the Chasseur jacket of the French Army. It hooked at the collar, and sloped away towards a short skirt (somewhat resembling that of a Light Infantryman's) which terminated it behind, had half facings; and on the shoulders, wings, made of interwoven rings.

Well pipeclayed doe or buck skins, fastened at the knee with buttons, and jack-boots with stiff tops, were worn.

A crimson sash encircled the waist, with a large "boss" or rose (from which the fringes depended) on the left side, in front, and the sash was tied behind under the coat with ribbons.

There was a framework or stiffening in the shabracque to keep the tassels from drooping.

See General Mercer's MS. Notes, pp. 49, 58, 62, 72.

AUTHORITIES.—Coloured print, title, "Sadler's Flying Artillery." 1798.
    Miniature of Officer R.H.A. Circa 1793.
    Water-colour sketch in Captain Lawson's "Evolutions of R.H.A." 1793.
    General Mercer's MS. Notes and description of uniform at this period.
    Prints of Light Dragoons in the "British Military Library." 1799.
    Prints of Light Infantry in the "British Military Library." 1799.

ROYAL HORSE ARTILLERY.

1793.

PLATE VIII.

AN OFFICER AND GUNNER, ROYAL ARTILLERY.

1794.

DESCRIPTION OF PLATE.

ON the left the Officer is shown wearing the curious head-dress of this period; his one epaulette denotes that he is a Company Officer, Field Officers wearing two.

The gunner is wearing his full-dress head-dress, from which was afterwards evolved the cap of the early part of the eighteenth century, and the chako of a later period.

AUTHORITIES.—For description see General Mercer's MS. Notes describing the uniform of the period.
Head-dress.—Portrait of Lieut.-General Congreve. Circa 1795.
Miniature of an Officer R.A. Circa 1795.

ROYAL ARTILLERY.

1794.

PLATE IX.

A GUNNER OF THE ROYAL ARTILLERY.

1797.

DESCRIPTION OF PLATE.

THE gunner of this period wore two cross-belts; one carried the bayonet, and the other the pouch. On the front of the one carrying the pouch was a hammer and pair of prickers for the vent of the gun.

A crimson cord ran along the centre of the belt, and from this depended a small powder-horn for priming the vent.

AUTHORITIES.—Coloured print, title, "Present Arms—First Motion." 1797.
Orders for dress as quoted in text.

ROYAL ARTILLERY.

1797.

PLATE X.

AN OFFICER AND GUNNER, ROYAL ARTILLERY.

1799.

Description of Plate.

The gunner is presenting arms to a Field Officer of this date.

The gunners had left off the long-tailed coats, and taken into wear single-breasted, short-tailed ones. It will be noticed that the Officer had an entirely different style of coat to that worn in Plate No. 8. It was double breasted, and the sword was carried depending from a shoulder-belt.

Authorities.—Coloured print, "Officer R.A.," in the "British Military Library." 1799.
    Portrait of Lieut.-General Congreve, R.A.
    Miniature of an Officer R.A.
    Water-colour sketches in "Artillery Movements," MS. drill-book. 1799.

ROYAL ARTILLERY.

1799.

PLATE XI.

AN OFFICER OF THE ROYAL HORSE ARTILLERY.

1815.

Description of Plate.

This represents the uniform worn during the Waterloo epoch for home service, as overalls worn over boots and breeches were usually the kit on foreign and active service. *Vide* Plate XII.

The Officers wore their sword-belts under the jacket, and attached to the sword by slings. It is interesting to compare this plate with No. 7, and to notice the difference between the jackets.

Very large blue shabracques with tassels, and stiffened with leather at the ends, were used.

Authorities.—Coloured print from Goddard's "Armies of Europe." 1812.
  Coloured print from "The Picturesque Representation of the Dress and Manners of the English." 1814.
  Coloured print from Beamish's "History of the King's German Legion." 1814.
  Coloured print from Hamilton Smith's "Military Costume of the British Empire."

ROYAL HORSE ARTILLERY.
1815.

PLATE XII.

TROOPER IN THE MOUNTED ROCKET CORPS OF THE ROYAL HORSE ARTILLERY.

1815.

Description of Plate.

This plate shows a trooper of the Rocket Corps: he is wearing the overalls, always worn on active service; they are buttoned on over his boots and breeches, and are chained down under the feet. His arms consist of a pistol and sabre, the latter being held in a frog, which was attached to the saddle.

The shabracque is stiffened with leather to keep it stretched.

Authorities.—Coloured plate from Congreve's "Rocket System." 1814.
  Two coloured prints, titles, "Artilleur Anglaise." Circa 1812.
  Coloured print from Hamilton Smith's "Military Costume of the British Empire." 1815.

ROYAL HORSE ARTILLERY.
Rocket Troop.
1815.

PLATE XIII.

AN OFFICER AND GUNNER, ROYAL ARTILLERY.

1815.

Description of Plate.

The Officer in the foreground is wearing the full-dress coatee of the period, white breeches, and Hessian boots.

This coatee is quite unique, and was worn for a very short time. The felt cap is a distinct feature of the Waterloo epoch. The dress of this period is decidedly a handsome one.

Authorities.—Full-dress coatee in R.A.I. Circa 1812.
    Portrait of Colonel Percy Drummond, R.A. Circa 1815.
    Engravings from Booth's "History of the Battle of Waterloo." 1815.
    Coloured print from Beamish's "History of the King's German Legion." 1814.
    Coloured print from Hamilton Smith's "Military Costume of the British Empire." 1815.

ROYAL ARTILLERY.
1815.

PLATE XIV.

AN OFFICER OF THE ROYAL ARTILLERY.

1820.

Description of Plate.

THE most remarkable feature to note in this plate is the change in the head-gear since Waterloo.

After having fought so long on the continent, and particularly against the French, the British Army had become greatly influenced by French fashions. The chako is distinctly of French origin, and the plate on it displays the old Board of Ordnance Arms. The Hessian boots with tassels were in vogue at this date.

AUTHORITIES.—Sketch entitled "The Garrison Staff, Woolwich." 1820.
Coloured print, "The Rotunda, Woolwich." 1820.

ROYAL ARTILLERY.

1820.

PLATE XV.

AN OFFICER OF THE ROYAL HORSE ARTILLERY.

1823.

DESCRIPTION OF PLATE.

BOOTS and breeches had been done away with since Plate XI.; Wellington boots and blue-grey overalls were now the fashion. The jacket was similar to that of the Waterloo period, as was also the helmet.

Shortly after this date the Horse Artillery helmet, which had been worn continuously since the formation of this branch of the service, was abolished, and a chako substituted instead of it. A cross-belt and sabretasche were also worn at this period.

AUTHORITIES.—Coloured print, Officer R.H.A. Heath, del. Published by Watson. 1820.

ROYAL HORSE ARTILLERY.
1823.

Plate XVI.

AN OFFICER OF THE ROYAL HORSE ARTILLERY.

1828.

Description of Plate.

Here is seen the Horse Artillery chako with its enormous waving plume, cap-lines, and flounders (as the tassels were termed).

The overalls were worn very loose, and pleated in round the waist.

The sword-belt was worn low down on the hips.

Barrelled sashes were the fashion at this date.

Authorities.—Coloured print, Officer R.H.A. Hull, del. 1828.
2 Coloured prints, Officers R.H.A., *Gentleman's Magazine of Fashion*. Heath, del. 1828.
Coloured print, Officer R.H.A. Heath, del. Circa 1829.
Print, "Artillerie Anglaise." Moltzheim, del. Circa 1830.
2 Coloured prints, R.H.A. Heath, del. Circa 1831.
2 Coloured prints, R.H.A. Martin, del. 1831.
Painting, Officer R.H.A. Drusheme, del. 1833.

ROYAL HORSE ARTILLERY.

1828.

PLATE XVII.

AN OFFICER AND GUNNER, ROYAL ARTILLERY.

1828.

DESCRIPTION OF PLATE.

THE grotesque appearance of the uniform at this time would be hard to beat.

Notice the wide-topped chako, with its enormous plume.

The trousers were worn very loose, and the coatees tight and high waisted.

AUTHORITIES.—2 Coloured prints, Officer and Gunner R.A. Hull, del. 1828.
    2 Coloured prints, Officer R.A., from *Gentleman's Magazine of Fashion*. Heath, del. 1828.
    Coloured print, title "Woolwich." Lami, del. 1829.
    Coloured print, Officer R.A. Heath, del. Circa 1829.
    Print, "Artillerie Anglaise." Moltzheim, del. Circa 1830.
    Coloured print, Royal Artillery. Heath, del. 1831.
    Coloured print, Royal Artillery. Martin, del. 1831.
    Water-colour sketch, "Gun Team R.A." 1835.

ROYAL ARTILLERY.

1828.

Plate XVIII.

AN OFFICER AND GUNNER, ROYAL ARTILLERY.

1840.

Description of Plate.

The figures here depicted wore one of the ugliest and most unserviceable uniforms ever invented by man.

This was the last year in which white trousers were worn; they were abolished in 1841.

The uniform of both Officers and men underwent very slight change since 1828.

This was the uniform worn at the time of Queen Victoria's accession.

Authorities.—Coloured print, "Royal Artillery." Heath, del. 1840.
Coloured print, "Guard-mounting, R.A." Hayes, del. 1840.
Orders of Dress as quoted in text.

ROYAL ARTILLERY.
1840.

PLATE XIX.

AN OFFICER OF THE ROYAL HORSE ARTILLERY.

1850.

Description of Plate.

This was the uniform worn by Officers of the Horse Artillery from about 1846 to the time of the Crimea. The chief difference between this plate and the last is the alteration in the head-gear from a chako to a bearskin busby, a jacket with five instead of three rows of buttons, and dark blue overalls instead of blue-grey.

The shabracque was also modernized.

Authorities.—Coloured print, Officer R.H.A. Giles, del. 1842.
    Two Coloured prints, Officers R.H.A. Jones, del. 1843–1845.
    Coloured print, R.H.A. Hayes, del. 1846.
    Coloured print, Officer R.H.A. Martens, del. 1844.
    Coloured prints, R.H.A. Campion, del. 1850.
    Coloured print, R.H.A. Martens, del. 1853.
    Coloured print, Officer R.H.A. Campion, 1854.
    Coloured print, R.H.A. 1855.
    R.H.A. jacket ⎫
       „ busby and plume ⎬ 1854. In R.A. Institution Museum.
       „ barrelled sash ⎭

ROYAL HORSE ARTILLERY.
1850.

PLATE XX.

A FIELD OFFICER AND GUNNER, ROYAL ARTILLERY.

1854.

Description of Plate.

It has already been stated that Queen Victoria's reign is divided into two epochs. This plate represents the uniform worn at the end of the first epoch.

For the last time are seen the chako, coatee with high collar, stock, and large epaulettes.

It will be noticed that waist-belts instead of cross-belts were worn, but otherwise the dress was similar to that of Plate XVIII.

AUTHORITIES.—Coloured print, Royal Artillery. Campion, del. 1850.
Coloured print, Royal Artillery. Martens. 1853.
Coloured print, Royal Artillery. 1855.
Coatee ⎫
Chako and plume ⎬ 1854. In R.A. Institution Museum.
Shoulder-belt and breastplate ⎪
Sword and sash ⎭

ROYAL ARTILLERY.

1854.

Plate XXI.

A FIELD OFFICER AND TRUMPETER OF THE ROYAL HORSE ARTILLERY.

1855—1871.

Description of Plate.

This plate represents the dress worn at the early part of the second epoch of Queen Victoria's reign, and differs widely from the last.

Very loose sleeves, low collars, and booted overalls were all features of this period. In fact, the style of dress was much more like that of the present day.

Long hair and bushy side-whiskers were fashionable at this time.

Authorities.—Photographs in R.A. Institution. 2 vols.
Uniform of the period in existence.
Dress Regulations, Royal Artillery. 1855.
Dress Regulations, Royal Artillery. 1864.

ROYAL HORSE ARTILLERY.

1855.

Plate XXII.

A FIELD OFFICER OF FIELD ARTILLERY AND A GUNNER OF GARRISON ARTILLERY.

1864.

DESCRIPTION OF PLATE.

WITH the exception of the difference between the Horse and Field Artillery, the style of dress is very similar to the last plate (No. XXI.). It is interesting to notice the old Artillery busby.

Contrasting the garrison gunner with the gunner in Plate XX., the difference in dress is most striking, the busby instead of the chako, and the tunic instead of the coatee.

AUTHORITIES.—Coloured print, "Officer R.A." Martens, del. 1855.
    Coloured print, "Royal Artillery." Thomas, del. 1861.
    Coloured print, "Royal Artillery." Sharpe, del. 1856.
    Photographs in R.A. Institution. 2 vols.
    Uniform of the period in existence.
    Dress Regulations, Royal Artillery. 1855.
    Dress Regulations, Royal Artillery. 1864.
    Dress Regulations for the Army. 1874.
    Plates in "Standing Orders of the Royal Regiment of Artillery." 1876.

ROYAL ARTILLERY.

1864.

Plate XXIII.

A CAPTAIN OF THE ROYAL HORSE ARTILLERY.

1893.

Description of Plate.

In Plate No. VII. was seen the uniform worn on the formation of the first troop of Horse Artillery, "the Chestnut Troop." Here is seen the same troop a century afterwards.

This was the uniform worn at the Queen's Diamond Jubilee, June 22, 1897.

Shabracques were worn on this occasion for the last time.

Authorities.—Studies from life.
Photographs of the period.
Uniform in existence.
"Dress Regulations for the Army." 1883.
"Dress Regulations for the Army." 1891.
"Dress Regulations for the Army." 1894.

ROYAL HORSE ARTILLERY.

1893.

PLATE XXIV.

A CAPTAIN OF GARRISON ARTILLERY, AND A LIEUTENANT OF FIELD ARTILLERY.

1897.

Description of Plate.

THE uniform of 1897 has undergone very slight alteration from that worn in Plate XXII., with the exception that helmets and jackboots have been substituted for busbies and booted overalls.

The collars of the tunic have become higher, and the sleeves tighter.

This was the uniform worn at the Diamond Jubilee.

AUTHORITIES.—Studies from life.
   Photographs of the period.
   Uniform in existence.
   "Dress Regulations for the Army."   1883.
   "Dress Regulations for the Army."   1891.
   "Dress Regulations for the Army."   1894.

ROYAL ARTILLERY.

1897.